Daily Dishonesty

THE BEAUTIFUL LITTLE LIES
WE TELL OURSELVES EVERY DAY

LAUREN HOM

Editor: Samantha Weiner
Designer: Danielle Young
Production Manager: Anet Sirna-Bruder

Library of Congress Control Number: 2014930734

ISBN: 978-1-4197-1403-0

Printed in the USA
10 9 8 7 6 5 4 3 2

Abrams Image books are available at special discounts when purchased in quantity for premiums
and promotions as well as fundraising or educational use. Special editions can also be created
to specification. For details, contact specialsales@abramsbooks.com or the address below.

115 West 18th Street
New York, NY 10011
www.abramsbooks.com

INTRODUCTION

October 9th, 2012 was a typical Tuesday night in my cozy East Village apartment: two bottles of wine (white for me, red for my roommate, Sophie), an assortment of cheeses, and two friends huddled around the kitchen table. Sophie and I were both beginning of our senior year at the School of Visual Arts, and between sips (and occasional gulps) of wine, our conversation turned—as it so often did—to the busy year ahead of us. Of course we talked about school, but we also talked about all the things we wanted to do in our spare time. "I'm going to brew my own beer," she said. "I want to go to yoga every day and learn how to make croissants," I replied, getting into the spirit of things. Suddenly, we looked at each other and burst out laughing. We realized we were both lying—neither of us actually had any free time! We were only one month into the school year, and we were already drowning in homework and design projects. These were just tiny, silly dreams that helped distract us and get us through the busy mazes of our lives.

As we giggled some more and polished off the cheese, I felt a lightbulb go off in my head. That night, I wrote down a dozen other small lies I regularly told myself, and then I started drawing. The next day, Daily Dishonesty was born.

As you read through this little book of lies, I hope that you're as guilty as we were, and that you can share a laugh about life's small (and sometimes large) trials and tribulations!

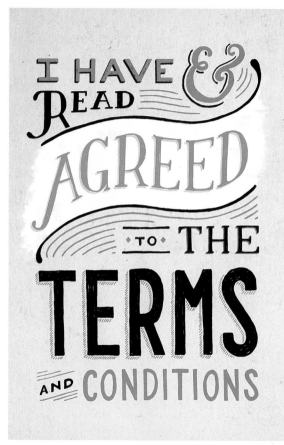

I LEARNED

MY LESSON

 I CAN

TRIM

 MY OWN

BANGS

I don't sunburn

This is just a

FAT MIRROR

I'M NOT

DRINKING

TONIGHT

I'LL BE THERE IN **5** MINUTES

I WANT TO BE **22** FOREVER

5 MINUTES OF FACEBOOK

6 A.M. YOGA

I'm TIRED
NOT hungover

I'LL GO TO BED

EARLY

TONIGHT

we can still be friends

IT'S NOT WHAT IT LOOKS LIKE

Sorry

I HAVE A BOYFRIEND

I DON'T LISTEN TO

MAINSTREAM

MUSIC

Things will be DIFFERENT this time

EVERYTHING
H·A·P·P·E·N·S
FOR A
REASON

Floss Everyday

Girls don't poop

IT WILL BE EASY

to cut out

CARBS

SHOPPING

COUNTS AS

CARDIO

I couldn't
EAT
Another
BITE

A
CUPCAKE
A DAY
keeps the
DOCTOR
AWAY

NO ROOM FOR DESSERT

I COULD DO IT

with my

EYES CLOSED

IT LOOKS

Better

ON YOU

I DON'T CARE IF YOU DATE MY

Ex-Boyfriend

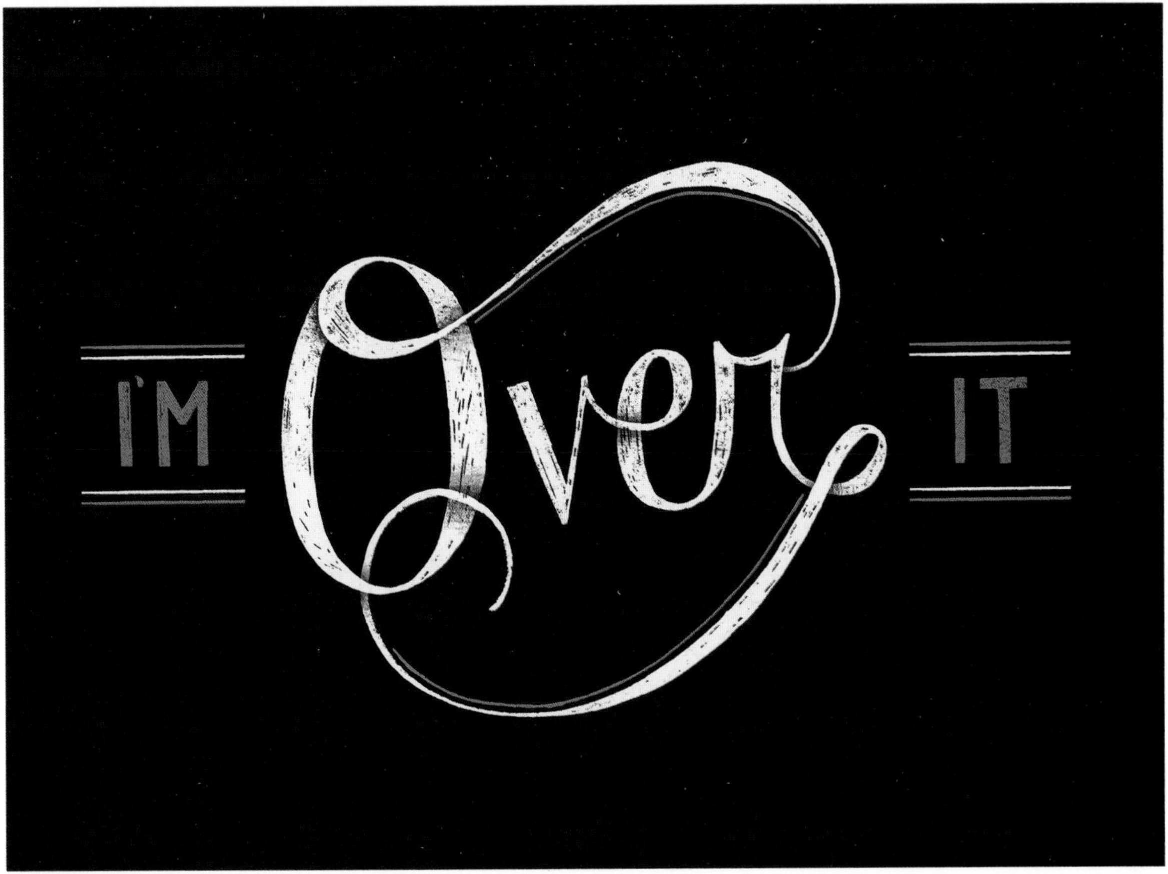
I'M
Over
IT

I WON'T
POP
THIS
PIMPLE

I LOVE MY
NEW
HAIRCUT

PORTION CONTROL

 I'LL JUST

REST MY

 Eyes

FOR A

SECOND

 I'LL Shower IN THE Morning

I'LL PUT ON

PANTS

TODAY

it WASN'T me

New Year's RESOLUTIONS

What happens in
VEGAS
Stays in
VEGAS

I WILL SAVE
HALF
— OF THIS —
PAYCHECK

I CAN'T...

I have to go

FEED MY CAT

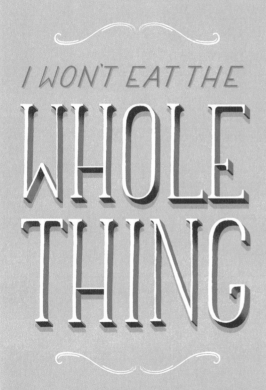

I'M NOT VERY

HUNGRY

I WON'T EAT
all of the
FRENCH FRIES

NO SNACKS
after dinner

NO, I'M NOT

Crying

THERE'S JUST

Something

IN MY

Eye

I WILL NOT

Drunk

Dial

MY EX

I AM NOT A *Jealous* PERSON

It's not *Your* *Fault*

I CAN HOLD MY Liquor

Mimosas are A GOOD SOURCE OF *Vitamin C*

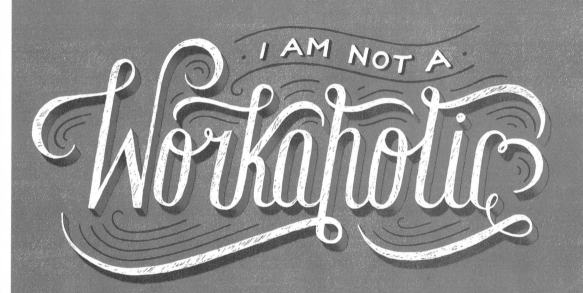

I'LL DO THE

DISHES

LATER

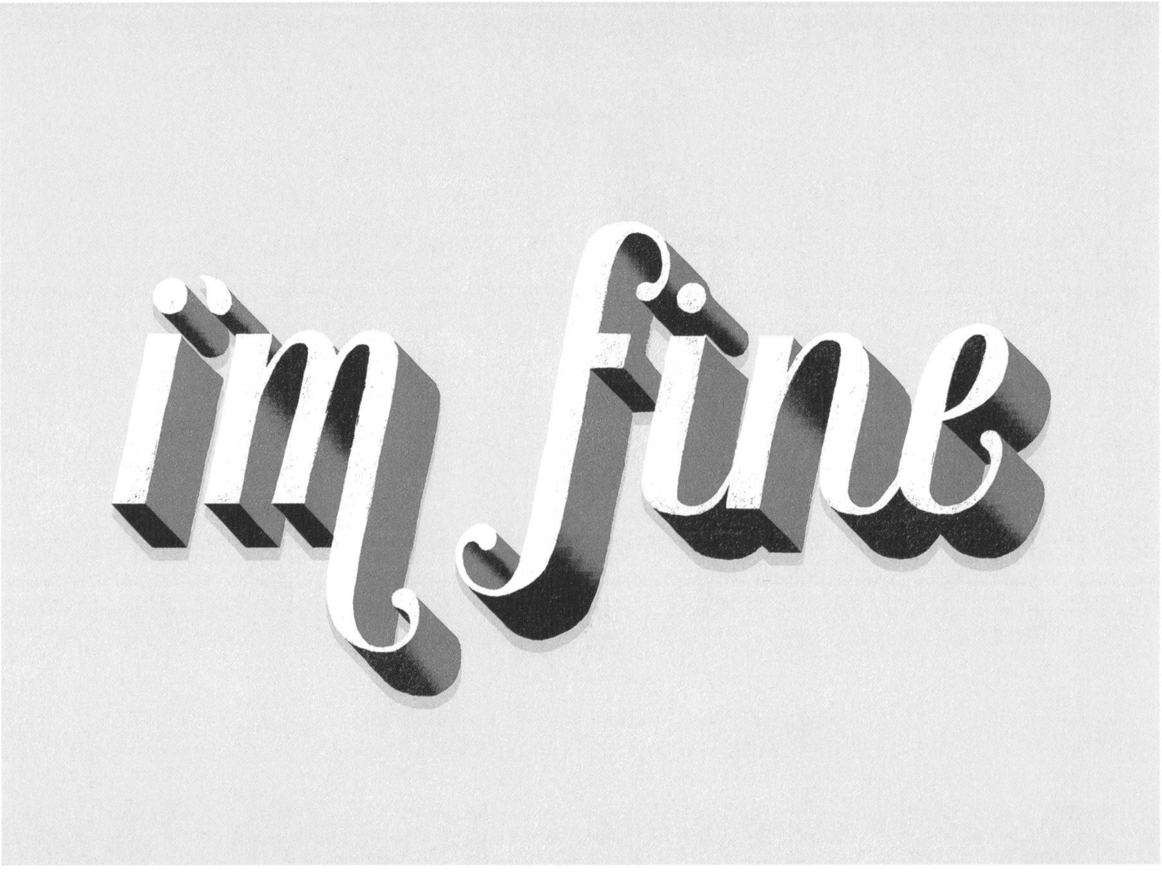
i'm fine

I'm too

OLD

for that

Just a Second

I WILL ONLY WATCH ONE EPISODE OF BREAKING BAD TONIGHT

I'LL JUST HAVE A SALAD

I'M NOT
ADDICTED
TO MY
PHONE

Sorry
MY PHONE
DIED

I CAN'T

BELIEVE

SHE JUST SAID THAT

Tequila

WAS A GOOD CHOICE

I DON'T GET Hangovers

TRUST ME

You won't

feel a thing

I KNOW exactly

how you FEEL

IF IT'S
BLACK
IT'S
FLATTERING

I'LL TRY NOT TO
JUDGE YOU
BY YOUR
SHOES

Leggings
COUNT AS
Pants

3 HOURS OF SLEEP IS ENOUGH

I WON'T PRESS Snooze

THIS STAYS *between* YOU AND ME

You have the
CUTEST BABY
I've ever seen

NO OFFENSE, BUT

I'm NEVER HAVING *Kids*

Side
SALAD

-OR-
French
FRIES

This cookie will go STRAIGHT TO MY BOOBS

THE BREAKUP WAS

MUTUAL

Make yourself at home

MY HOUSE IS USUALLY CLEANER THAN THIS

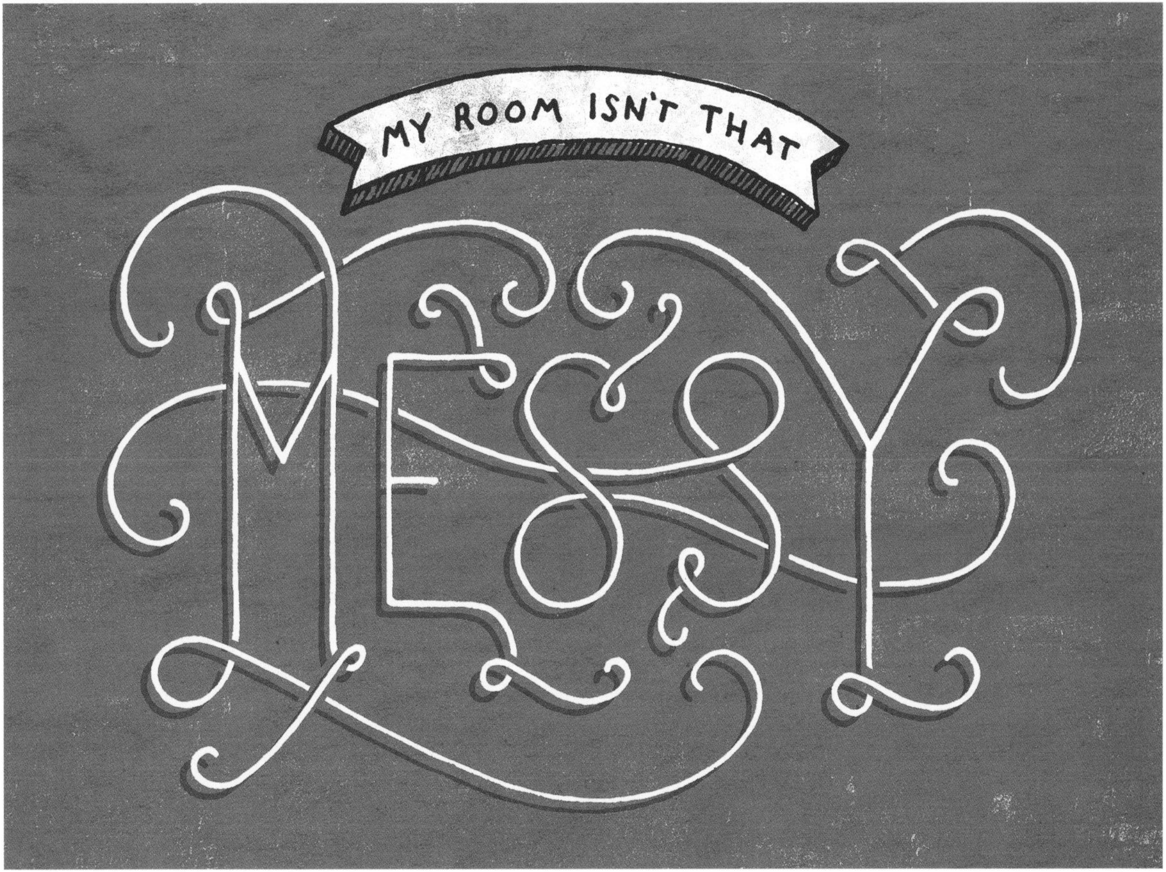
MY ROOM ISN'T THAT
MESSY

IT WON'T RAIN TODAY

CAKE

≈ *is mostly* ≈

AIR

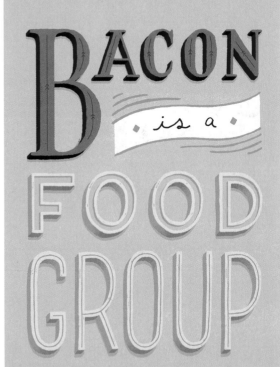

BACON

is a

FOOD GROUP

PIZZA

IS A

VEGETABLE

HIGH

Heels

IN BROOKLYN

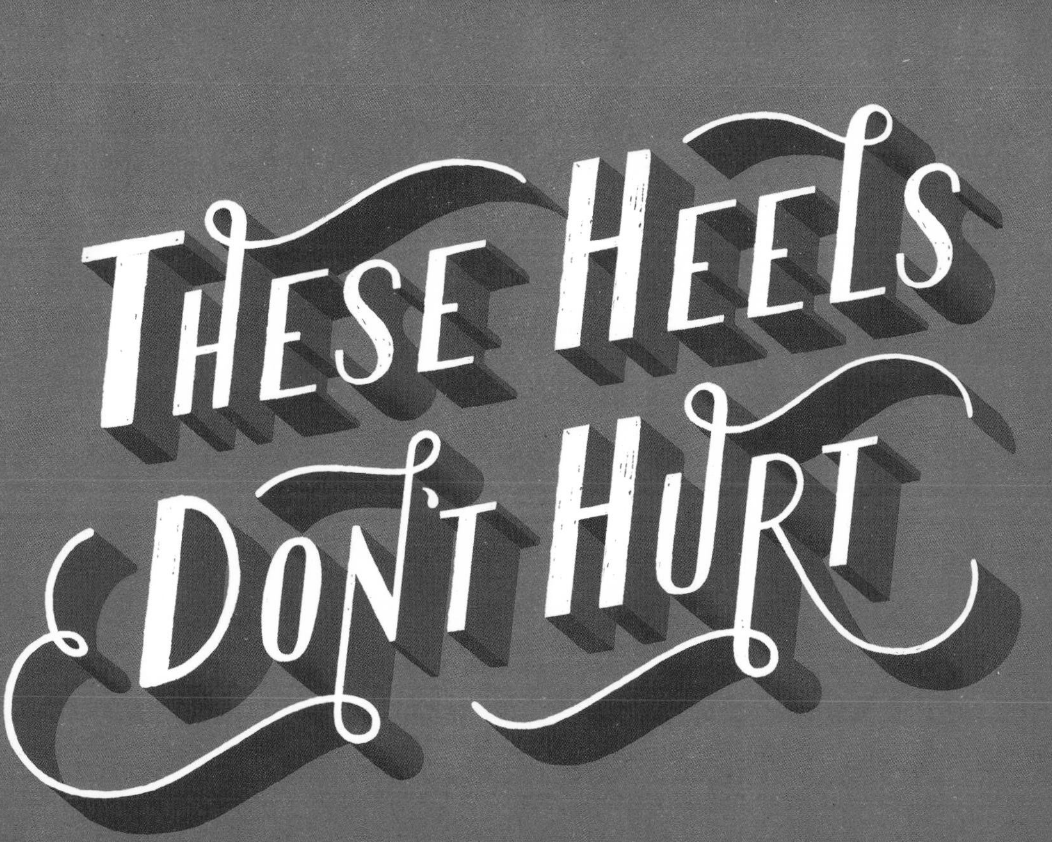
These Heels
Don't Hurt

Calories don't count

ON THE WEEKEND

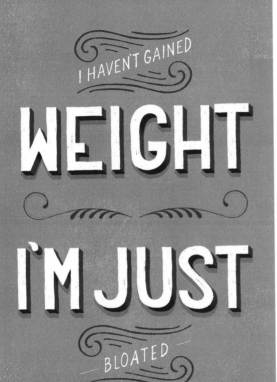

I HAVEN'T GAINED

WEIGHT

I'M JUST

BLOATED

THE

LOW-FAT

VERSION

TASTES JUST AS GOOD

— TODAY —

I'LL PULL IT

TOGETHER

I WILL ONLY HAVE

ONE

glass

— OF —

WINE

TONIGHT

I'm Never Drinking Again

I CAN **DRINK MORE** THAN YOU

I ONLY **Smoke** WHEN I **Drink**

ACKNOWLEDGMENTS

I'd like to thank all of the lovely people who helped make this book happen:

Sophia Erskine, my fellow wine and cheese enthusiast, for her words of wisdom and exceptional eye for layouts.

Becca Luce, my best friend, for unconditionally loving and supporting me since the eighth grade.

My fabulous friends, for being the inspiration for half of the content in this book. I promise that's a compliment.

My family, for putting up with my weird self for the past twenty-three years.

Gail Anderson, my favorite teacher and mentor, for helping me discover my point of view as a designer and *always* pushing me in the right direction.

Katherine Latshaw, my lovely literary agent, for discovering my blog and giving me the best twenty-second birthday present.

Rebecca, Samantha, Danielle, and the rest of my amazing team at Abrams, for their expertise in putting together the prettiest book of lies I've ever seen (if there are even any other books of lies).

And a final thank you to all of my followers and fans who have supported the blog since day one. I wish I could give each and every one of you an awkwardly long hug.